I0748649

THE CLARITY ALMANAC

The Clarity Almanac

---

by Tasha Monroe

2026 EDITION — FIRE HORSE YEAR

THE CLARITY ALMANAC: 2026 Edition — Fire Horse Year

Published by **Edyn House Press**,
an imprint of **Simply Edyn & Co., LLC**
United States of America

ISBN: 979-8-9942615-0-7

Cover and interior design by **Edyn House Press**
First Edition, 2026

Printed on demand in the United States of America and other locations.

Dedication

For anyone who feels there has to be more to life than just getting through it, even when getting through it takes everything you have.

For those who try to move gently through the world, with intention and a quiet, stubborn hope that what they do still matters.

If you're here, especially on the hard days, this book was written for you, by someone walking beside you, not ahead of you.

Contents

Opening Note from Author 15

Fire Horse Year 21

Heart of the Work 32

How to Use This (or: How to Be With It) 37

Monthly Themes 41

- January: *A Start That Minds Its Business (And Lets You Mind Yours)* 43
- February: *The Honest Inventory* 46
- March: *The Shift You Can't Outsmart* 50
- April: *Standing Where Your Life Actually Is* 54
- May: *The Line You (Hopefully) Stop Moving* 58
- June: *Letting Yourself Be Helped (On Purpose, Not by Accident)* 61
- July: *The Quiet Bravery of Not Bolting* 65
- August: *The Polite Refusal To Lose Yourself* 69
- September: *When The Math Starts Mathing* 72
- October: *The Clearing That Tells The Truth* 77

The Season That Tells On Us 81

- November: *The Year In Its Real Clothes* 84
- December: *After All That* 88

Quarterly Check-Ins 93

Closing Manifesto 99

Reciprocity Principles 103

Building Your Circle 107

Finding Your Voice 115

Carrying the Year Forward 119

The Body Is Not a Detour 123

Note for the Hard Days 129

Closing Note from Author 131

Acknowledgment 139

About the Author 142

Opening Note from the Author

This year will likely be remembered. And not from a distance.

We have been living inside it long enough to understand that this isn't a passing phase. Somewhere along the way something steady stopped feeling steady. Conversations carry more tension than they used to. Decisions feel heavier. Things you once tolerated without thinking now sit in your chest longer. What you once called "normal" doesn't quite fit the way it did.

It's not only tension. It's fatigue. The effort of staying informed without becoming numb. The discipline of holding onto your values when they feel inconvenient. Survival and dignity are no longer assumed. They are being weighed, challenged, and, in some places, stripped back.

For some communities, this is not new. For others, it is the first crack in something they thought would last.

There hasn't been time to absorb what this shift means. The world hasn't slowed down so we can make sense of it. What's unfolding won't wait to be understood. And still, life is asking to be lived. Meals cooked. Emails answered. Children raised. Work done.

The real work is not forecasting what comes next. It is staying present inside what is already here—without withdrawing from the life you are still responsible for.

Recognizing tension before it becomes undeniable is not overreaction. It is awareness. It comes from learning to read the room before the room admits what it is. That kind of clarity does not arrive suddenly. It is earned. It is practiced.

It also runs against the grain of the world we inhabit.

We live inside systems that reward speed. Quick reactions. Decisions made without consequence literacy. Confidence delivered on cue. What they rarely reward is careful thinking. Discernment.

Most days, we're pushed to decide before we've had time to reflect, to take a position before we've had space to notice what we actually believe, to speak with certainty even when something inside us hasn't settled yet.

This almanac is not an argument against engagement. It is an invitation to steadiness.

Discernment cannot be rushed without distortion, and a life lived entirely in reaction is not the same as a life lived deliberately.

Eventually, that pace stops working. Not because of one dramatic event, but because the answers that once steadied us no longer do. They still sound fine when repeated out loud; they just don't survive contact with real days.

If you feel unsettled, it may not be confusion. It may be the effort it takes to stay honest, to keep your thinking flexible, to resist becoming someone you no longer recognize.

The last decade reshaped how we trust, decide and assess risk, not through a single rupture, but through sustained pressure. Loss layered on loss. Disruptions that never fully resolved. Achievements that arrived without the relief they promised.

So now many of us carry mixed signals at once: confidence and doubt, hope and fatigue, insight and hesitation. That doesn't mean something is wrong. It usually means you've been paying attention.

A new year doesn't always feel like a reset. It feels more like a threshold you can step across when you're ready, not to reinvent yourself, not to perform transformation, just to take an honest look at what you've been sustaining and what it has been asking of you in return.

What matters now? What do you already know but haven't said out loud? What needs to end, even if it once made sense? What keeps asking for room?

If you're here, you're not looking for instructions. You're looking to think clearly inside the life you already have.

That's where *The Clarity Almanac* comes in.

This isn't a set of answers. It's a practice, a place to strengthen judgment, to notice how you decide, to create space between what happens and how you respond.

There is no performance of self-improvement here. No pressure to become someone new. This work is not about fixing yourself. It is about staying with yourself, especially in the space between what you planned and what actually happened.

You are allowed to think slowly in a fast world. You are allowed to question what once felt settled. You are allowed to want a fuller life without pretending you've figured it all out.

Clarity rarely arrives as an announcement. It builds quietly in how you decide, what you decline, what you're willing to wait for. Over time, that steadiness becomes self-respect. Not bravado. Not certainty. Just trust in your own attention.

This work matters because it keeps you awake inside your life, not reactive, not rigid, present.

Let this be a place where your thinking grows less punishing, where your inner dialogue becomes more honest and compassionate, where you practice staying instead of rushing.

A fuller life isn't built by having all the answers. It's built by living well inside the questions.

Maybe that's what this year is asking for. Not perfection. Not certainty. Just presence, attention, honesty, a willingness to stay.

An honest life is built by staying with yourself, especially when certainty falls apart.

— Tasha

The Fire Horse Year

Some years do not simply add to your life. They change the conversation you are having with yourself entirely. This feels like one of those years.

Not because of superstition. Not because of performance. And not because we need symbolism to explain what already feels unsettled. It feels that way because many of us are standing in front of questions we can no longer avoid. Questions about our lives, our choices and the compromises we made to survive that no longer feel honest. This is the kind of year when inconvenient truths stop feeling optional.

In the Chinese zodiac, 2026 is a Yang Fire Horse year, a rare alignment that occurs once every sixty years. The Horse represents movement, independence, endurance and willpower. It is associated with momentum, instinct and an intolerance for confinement. The element of Fire intensifies whatever it touches. It illuminates, accelerates and exposes. When Fire overlays the Horse, individualism sharpens, stagnation becomes combustible and what has been quietly unstable is brought into the open.

The last Fire Horse year was 1966. That year marked the beginning of China's Cultural Revolution, a radical upheaval that challenged entrenched authority structures. The Vietnam War escalated, reshaping global politics and domestic unrest in the United States. Youth movements expanded. The Black Power movement intensified. Around the world, institutions that had once seemed durable began to show fracture lines. The zodiac did not cause these events, but the symbolism aligns with the pattern: prolonged pressure meeting ignition.

Fire Horse years do not invent instability. They reveal it. They coincide with moments when inherited narratives lose credibility and individuals begin withdrawing their quiet cooperation from systems that no longer make sense.

You feel the pattern already. It appears in the slow erosion of trust. In institutions that no longer inspire confidence but demand compliance. In conversations that once felt procedural and now feel personal. In the realization that "normal" was sustained less by stability and more by collective agreement.

The Element of Fire

movement • illumination • refinement • instinct • disruption that serves a purpose

The element of Fire is often misunderstood as destruction alone. It is also illumination. It burns away what has already lost integrity. It clarifies edges. It makes avoidance more difficult to sustain. In lived experience, Fire looks less like noise and more like insistence: the truth that keeps surfacing, the fatigue of pretending something still works, the recognition that staying the same now carries greater cost than moving.

It exposes what's been pushed aside. It calls bluff on avoidance. It doesn't force change. It just makes self-deception harder to maintain.

In real life, Fire doesn't always arrive dramatically. It shows up as:

- the irritation that won't resolve
- the question that keeps following you around the room
- the truth you finally admit to yourself at 2 a.m. when no one is listening
- the decision you make because staying the same now costs more than moving

Fire isn't asking you to reinvent yourself. It stops letting you pretend as efficiently.

Here, Fire becomes a way of reading yourself more honestly—paying attention to where you pull back, where you tense, and where something in you keeps insisting forward despite your attempts to override it.

The Archetype of the Horse

freedom • endurance • direction • self-determination • momentum • sovereignty

The Horse doesn't move to prove anything. It moves because something inside says *now*.

The Horse represents forward motion. It is endurance without sacrifice and direction without permission, forward motion that does not need an audience. . It does not move to prove itself. It moves because confinement becomes intolerable. In a Fire Horse year, that archetype becomes personal. Where have you been shrinking to preserve stability? Where have you negotiated with your own clarity? Where has resilience quietly turned into self-erasure?

In a year shaped by this kind of reflection, the Horse points to the part of you that already knows when shrinking has stopped working. The strength you forget is yours because you've been too busy meeting everyone else's expectations. The direction that becomes visible the moment you stop auditioning for your own life.

The Horse doesn't erase its past. It carries its history forward. That's what gives its movement credibility.

Your journal becomes the reins—not to restrain you, but to help you steer with intention instead of apology.

When Fire and Horse Come Together

The convergence of Fire and Horse historically aligns with periods when institutions lose unquestioned authority, movements gain speed and private dissatisfaction becomes public language. In personal life, the shift is often quieter. It appears as recalibration—the decision to withdraw cooperation from parts of your life that no longer align, not dramatically or publicly, but internally.

The work of a Fire Horse year is not forecasting what comes next. It is staying present within what is already here without abandoning the life you remain responsible for. It is recognizing tension before it becomes collapse. It is practicing discernment in a culture that rewards speed over consequence literacy and confidence delivered on cue over careful thinking.

The mistake would be assuming that such a year demands grand gestures. It does not. It demands precision and the willingness to seek clarity in better aligned questions.

A Fire Horse year asks clearer questions:

- What are you still tolerating?
- What beliefs have stayed out of habit, not

conviction?
• What no longer fits?
• Where have you mistaken endurance for alignment?.

This book isn't here to predict outcomes or promise resolution. It's here to support honest, sustainable noticing—especially in the places where denial has been doing the heavy lifting.

The monthly themes are shaped by this principle: movement that reflects consent, honesty that doesn't require self-punishment, courage without performance. Your journal becomes the place where truth can land before it gets reshaped into something more acceptable.

Why This Year Matters Now

This almanac is not intended to mystify this year. It is meant to help you navigate it. The monthly themes are structured around movement without self-abandonment, courage without theatrics, truth without cruelty and endurance without erasure. The journal becomes a place to measure movement against intention.

For a long time, many of us have been living in a state of managed survival. Adapting. Absorbing. Adjusting. Staying functional inside systems that kept shifting under our feet.

None of it showed up as one dramatic emergency. It built slowly. Economic strain that lingered longer than expected. Political instability that felt constant. Social division that changed the tone of everyday life. A kind of low-grade uncertainty that just stayed on in the background. Over time, we adjusted. We learned how to keep going. How to stay useful. How to remain composed, sometimes all at once.

It left many of us tired in ways sleep couldn't fix.

What we call burnout, anxiety, confusion, or loss of direction did not come from personal failure. It's the cost of living for too long in conditions that were never meant to be permanent.

Survival mode did what it was supposed to do. It narrowed focus. It muted instinct. It deferred desire. It helped people get through. But it also came with a cost.

Over time, many of us stopped asking honest questions because we were busy managing the next demand. We benched dreams not because they disappeared, but because they felt impractical. We learned how to tolerate lives that were livable, even when they were no longer true.

This year matters because those strategies are reaching their limit.

The ways you kept yourself intact aren't wrong. They just aren't enough anymore. The habits that helped you endure are asking to be examined. Not condemned. Not torn down overnight. Just named.

That's why reflection becomes necessary—not as self-correction, but as orientation. A way to step out of reflex and back into authorship.

This isn't a call to dramatic change. It's a call to clear-eyed truth. To see what you've been carrying. To see what no longer fits, even if it once did.

Clarity here isn't indulgent. It's stabilizing. It allows you to stop confusing endurance with alignment. It helps you recognize where you've been operating on borrowed momentum instead of real consent.

Set aside symbolism and what remains is this: if something in your life has reached its limit, clarity will surface whether you welcome it or not. Fire does not demand chaos. It demands honesty. The Horse does not demand escape. It demands direction.

The assignment for this year is not reinvention for its own sake. It is alignment. If you were not negotiating with fear, what would you move toward? That question is the work of this year.

The Cost of Survival Becoming a Lifestyle

The last decade taught many of us how to endure. What it didn't teach us was how to come back.

We learned how to stay functional in chaos. How to keep moving with a tight jaw and a steady face. How to call exhaustion "strength" and grief "gratitude." We learned how to be impressive under pressure. Useful. Reliable. The person others could count on when things fell apart.

What we didn't learn was how to rest without explaining ourselves. Or how to want something simply because we wanted it.

Survival is effective. But it is not neutral.

It shapes what you choose. It narrows what you imagine is possible. It teaches you to favor safety over truth, tolerance over closeness, stability over the parts of you that were never meant to be postponed forever. Over time, a smaller life can begin to look like the responsible one.

Many people don't realize what survival has cost them until their systems are still braced, still alert, long after the emergency has passed. That's often when the grief arrives—not only for what happened, but for who you had to become in order to keep going.

This is why this year matters.

The shift has already begun. You may notice it in the questions that won't settle. In the choices that once felt necessary but now feel strangely hollow. In relationships that asked you to stay composed instead of honest. In roles that rewarded your competence without ever offering care. In versions of yourself built for endurance, not for a life that could hold pleasure, ease, or rest.

The Fire Horse year doesn't ask for reinvention. It asks for retrieval.

Not a dramatic exit. Not a public declaration. But a turning back toward what was set aside so you could survive. The instincts you learned to ignore. The longings you called impractical. The limits you kept bending to keep things smooth.

Choosing yourself in this season doesn't announce itself. It looks specific. It looks like noticing when resilience has turned into self-erasure—and deciding, without spectacle, to stop cooperating with that arrangement.

That isn't rebellion. It's self-possession returning.

The Fire Horse Principle

If you set the symbolism aside, what remains is simple and exact:

This is a year to choose yourself with fewer explanations.

That choice is rarely dramatic. It doesn't look reckless or loud. It looks like care. It looks like discernment. It looks like a form of self-respect that allows you to stay intact rather than disappear.

This book isn't here to decide anything for you. It's here to help you notice what your life has been trying to say beneath the noise—under the deadlines, the expectations, the version of you others have grown accustomed to. The knowing you've learned to override because everything else demanded your attention first.

Before we begin, that's the only thing you need to remember: You already carry more clarity than you've been giving yourself credit for.

This work is simply here to help you listen again.

The Heart of the Work:

Voice, Action, Community

There's a familiar story we've been told about the last decade. That it made us stronger. That the struggle was instructive. I don't think those years were meant to be proof of strength. I think they just left their mark.

Some of us came out with clearer lines. Some with quieter lives. Some with a kind of tired that doesn't fully go away. Most of us are still making sense of what shifted, even if we haven't found the language for it yet.

This almanac isn't here to make any of that more palatable. It's here because pretending everything is fine has never led to wholeness. The Fire Horse year doesn't ask you to rise to the occasion or perform resilience one more time.

It asks something simpler, and harder: tell the truth. To yourself first. And then, slowly, in the places where you live, work, love, and try to belong.

And that has consequences.

Truth is hard. Harder than many people have the nerve to say out loud. Not because it is complicated. Because it costs something.

It costs comfort. It costs approval. It costs the version of normal you have been trying to preserve even as it quietly stops working. Most people do not resist truth because they cannot see it. They resist it because they understand what it will require.

This is what a Fire Horse year asks of us.

It isn't about chaos or theatrics. It's about the quiet admission that some things in your life no longer hold up under honest scrutiny. The job that keeps costing you more than it gives back. The relationship you keep adjusting yourself to fit. The version of stability you've been defending out of habit more than belief. It's about noticing that and deciding what you're no longer willing to carry.

Fire does not invent tension. It exposes it. It brings heat to what has been sitting dormant. It illuminates the cracks that were already there and asks whether you plan to keep pretending they are not structural.

That adjustment is rarely loud. It is the boundary you stop apologizing for. The sentence you let yourself finish without softening it. The moment you realize you are tired of shrinking so other people do not have to adjust.

If you feel tension before it becomes undeniable, you are not dramatic. You are paying attention. That kind of awareness is earned. It comes from living long enough inside systems to recognize when they begin to strain.

We do not talk enough about the intelligence people carry through ordinary days. The way instincts sharpen when institutions wobble. The way people sense patterns before there is clean language for them. The way communities quietly rearrange themselves when stability cannot be counted on. That kind of knowing is not abstract. It is lived. It is built over time. And it deserves respect.

Most meaningful change does not start with an announcement. It starts when someone understands themselves differently. Reflection is not indulgence. It is orientation. Paying attention to your own experience is how you remain present inside it. Not checking out. Not moving on autopilot. Actually participating in your life.

This book is for people who know when something no longer fits, even if they cannot fully explain why. People who are perceptive and capable, and often more tired than they let on. People who have tried effort, optimism or discipline and discovered that none of it holds without honesty.

If that is you, you do not need a dramatic overhaul. You need steadiness. A place to think clearly from.

And you are not meant to do that alone.

Real community is not built through perfect agreement. It is built through proximity and reciprocity. Through the shared understanding that human beings need one another, especially when things feel uncertain. We are meant to be witnessed, supported, gently challenged and held with care.

Finding your people is not about popularity. It is about noticing who sees you clearly, who stays curious about your growth and who reminds you that you do not have to carry everything by yourself. It is also about becoming someone who can offer that same steadiness in return.

None of us moves through life without causing harm. That is part of being human. But awareness changes what comes next. Awareness creates responsibility. Responsibility, held with compassion, shapes culture, even in small circles. Especially in small circles.

You are not being asked to become a symbol or a solution. You are being asked to stay. With yourself.

With others. With the truth of who you are and what you are capable of building in relationship.

So when this year asks you to speak, to reach out, to say no, to say yes, to let something go or to try again, understand that it is not spectacle. It is life asking for your attention.

Do not disappear. Do not shrink back into the version of yourself that survived the past but cannot imagine the future. Stay present in the ways you can. Stay connected to people who want to build with integrity and care.

There is more capacity in you than you have probably been taught to recognize. Not because you need to become someone else, but because you have already endured more than you give yourself credit for.

And the people meant to walk with you will recognize it when they see it.

How to Use This (or: How to Be With It)

Before anything else, let's name what this is *not*.

This is not a program. It is not a curriculum. It is not here to manage you, optimize you, or turn your life into something neat and presentable.

If "guide" feels like too strong a word, that's intentional. This book does not lead from the front. It walks beside you. It offers structure without pressure and shape without control. Think of it less as instruction and more as a tool you can reach for when you need help hearing yourself again.

You can move through these pages daily, weekly, monthly, or only when something in you starts to feel thin or stretched. There is no correct pace here. There is only the pace that tells the truth about your life.

Let this be a place you return to when the world feels too loud to sort out what you actually feel. A place where you can notice what's shifting inside you before someone else rushes in to name it for you. A place where your inner life is allowed to take up space without being edited for someone else's comfort.

Each month includes a theme, a short reflection, and a set of prompts. They are not assignments. They are not proof that you are "doing the work." They are invitations. Some will open something quietly. Some will slow you down. Some will land with a clear *yes*. Others may feel premature, irritating, or simply irrelevant. That is not failure. That is discernment.

Reflection isn't linear. Take what speaks to you and leave what doesn't. Come back later if something begins to tug at you. If a sentence lingers, mark it. If a question unsettles you, sit with it gently. You are allowed to move in circles.

The quarterly check-ins are simply pauses. They exist so you can look at your direction without urgency or judgment. They hold the kinds of questions most of us postpone until we're already exhausted: Is the way I'm spending my time aligned with the life I say I want? What have I been avoiding? What actually deserves more of me right now?

These moments aren't about performance. They're about integrity. Yours.

If you're pairing this book with a journal, let them speak to each other. Let your journal hold what's unfinished, contradictory, or raw. Let it carry the scribbles, the half-sentences, the late-night honesty. Let this book hold the framework. One is the conversation. The other is the container.

If you're using this on its own, it will still meet you fully. Reflection doesn't depend on format. It depends on willingness. The willingness to look at your life without flinching. Without shrinking your needs. Without pretending you're fine when you're not.

Give yourself permission to be surprised by what you notice. Give yourself permission to move slowly in a culture that rewards speed. Give yourself permission not to know yet.

You are not completing a task. You are building a relationship with yourself.

This is not a race. It's a season. You're allowed to grow at a pace that honors your capacity, your history, and your hunger for what feels real.

Approach these pages the way you would approach a conversation with someone who genuinely cares about your well-being: honestly, without performance, and with care. Let this be something you return to when everything else feels like too much. Let it offer space when you've been compressing yourself just to get through.

Change rarely arrives through grand declarations. It shows up through small, steady choices made by someone willing to live truthfully.

The rest will meet you when you're ready.

And when it does, you'll meet it as yourself—not as the version you once thought you had to be.

Monthly Themes

Each month in this collection is anchored by a single theme. Not as a rule or a directive, but as an orientation. Something to lean into. A gentle nudge toward a line of inquiry worth your attention. These themes are meant to meet you where you are, not where you think you should be. Some will feel immediate. Others will unfold slowly, revealing themselves only after you've lived with them awhile. That's not a flaw in the process. It's the point.

Inside each month, you'll find an opening essay, a set of reflection prompts, and a small selection of practices. The essay is there to set the tone and offer context. The prompts are meant to sharpen your noticing, not rush you toward conclusions. The practices are optional and adaptable, designed to flex with your life rather than compete with it. Nothing here requires completion, consistency, or performance. You are free to read straight through, skip ahead, return later, or linger where something catches.

Think of the monthly themes as a framework, not a schedule. You might stay with one theme for a few days, or carry it across an entire season. You might write through every prompt, or simply keep a single sentence with you as you move through your days. Take what resonates. Leave what doesn't. This work isn't about keeping up. It's about staying present in a way that feels honest, humane, and sustainable for you.

JANUARY — A START THAT MINDS ITS BUSINESS (AND LETS YOU MIND YOURS)

January has a reputation for being decisive, but most of the time it shows up more like an uninvited supervisor—standing over your shoulder, asking what your plan is, as if certainty arrives on demand. The calendar resets, yes, but the rest of you might still be untangling last year's knots, sorting through half-finished thoughts, or simply trying to remember what day it is. This isn't failure; it's human biology doing its best.

The world loves a dramatic reboot. It loves the illusion that all you need is a clean slate and a positive attitude. But you live in the real world. You carry memory, experience, fatigue, longing, resistance, hope—none of which evaporate at midnight. So January, in its better moments, offers something far more useful: a beginning that doesn't ask you to pretend. A beginning that minds its own business and gives you room to mind yours.

This month isn't about reinventing yourself on command. It's about noticing where you actually are before you start marching anywhere. Notice the honest signals—what's tugging at you, what's settling, what's stirring—and let that shape your direction. You don't need to be ready. You just need to be willing to tell the truth.

If there's anything optimistic here, it's this: beginnings don't require theatrics. They require honesty, and you already have that available. So start where you are. Not where the marketing campaigns think you should be. Not where your past self-promised you'd land. Right here, in the version of your life that exists today.

The year will meet you there.

Reflection Prompts for January

1. **If you strip away expectation—yours, theirs, the world's—where do you actually find yourself at the start of this year?**
   Let the answer be unpolished.
2. **What part of last year is still tapping you on the shoulder, and what might it be trying to tell you if you weren't rushing past it?**
3. **If you gave yourself permission to move into this year without urgency, what possibilities—small or subtle—start to appear?**

Practice for January — A Practice of Settling the Ground

Choose one evening this month to slow down long enough to take stock without judgment. Turn down the noise—not because it's noble, but because it's necessary if you want to hear yourself think.

Sit with a notebook or a blank page and ask:

- What do I need more of?
- What do I need less of?
- What is asking to be noticed?
- What is asking to be released?

Don't force insight. Don't try to manufacture motivation.

Just listen. Most beginnings don't arrive with fireworks.
They arrive with a sentence you finally admit, a decision you no longer avoid, a truth you can no longer unsee.

That counts. It always has.

FEBRUARY — THE HONEST INVENTORY

February has a way of exposing what January politely ignored. Once the collective enthusiasm for "new beginnings" fizzles out, you're left with the far less glamorous task of noticing what actually stayed. And honestly, February is excellent at this—not because it's profound, but because it has no patience for theatrics.

This is the month when last year's leftovers step back into frame: the habits that keep tagging along, the attachments that insist on being acknowledged, the desires you thought you strategically out-organized. They don't care about your calendar. They care about truth, which makes February inconvenient in the most productive way.

The point isn't to judge any of it. The point is to stop performing neutrality. Some things linger because they need tending. Some linger because you keep pretending you're fine. And some linger simply because you haven't paused long enough to ask whether they still belong.

But here's the part February rarely gets credit for: it's also the first month that shows you the weight you've normalized. Especially if you come from a background—or a century, frankly—where support was unreliable, inconsistent, or conditional, the instinct is predictable: carry it yourself, don't complain, keep moving. That form of endurance is impressive, but it's not sustainable. And more importantly, it's not always yours to hold.

February isn't asking you to drop everything. It's asking you to tell the truth about what you're carrying and how long you've been carrying it without help. Because later in the year—June, specifically—you'll be invited into a different sort of courage: the courage to let some of it be witnessed, shared, or released.

This month simply plants the seed. Notice the weight. Name its history. Acknowledge the part of you that calls exhaustion "normal."

That's the beginning of discernment—the kind that doesn't need to announce itself, because it's busy doing the work.

This month asks one question: What is following you into the rest of the year—and what might change shape if you let it?

Prompts for February

1. **What truth has been quietly forming beneath all your distractions—and why might it finally be**

ready for you to hear it?
Truth doesn't vanish; it waits.

2. **Which parts of your life feel heavier than you admit—and where did you first learn that you had to carry them alone?**
Endurance has a lineage.

3. **What no longer fits who you're becoming, even if you can't articulate the alternative yet?**
Discomfort is an early compass.

4. **If you loosened your grip on something you've held for too long, what fear surfaces—and what desire sits directly behind that fear?**
Fear is often guarding the very thing you want.

5. **What longing keeps resurfacing with a steady, calm persistence—and what would it mean to take it seriously?**
Some desires are simply tired of waiting for your permission.

Practice for February — The Honest Sorting

Set aside a moment when the house, the world, and your internal narrator are still enough to let you hear yourself think.

Write three headings:

Keep. Loosen. Let Go.

Then, without editorializing, place the pieces of your life—habits, routines, hopes, obligations, roles, beliefs, grudges, ambitions—under whichever category your body answers "yes" to before your mind negotiates.

Do not rationalize. Do not defend. Do not argue with yourself. Just place each thing where it naturally lands.

Put the page away for a week. When you return, notice what still feels true and what shifted in your absence.

This exercise isn't about decisiveness. It's about learning the early language of your own discernment—and recognizing the weight you were never meant to carry alone.

MARCH — THE SHIFT YOU CAN'T OUTSMART

March is famous for one thing: ending the charade. All the polite avoidance, the elegant procrastination, the long-winded explanations you've been giving yourself —March shortens them into a single sentence:

Are you doing this or not?

NOTE: Before we go any further, let's be clear: this isn't a dismissal of the progress you *have* made. You've earned your wins. You've followed through on things you once only dreamed about. You've held your life together through layers of stress no one saw—unless, of course, they caught the way your eye twitched every time someone said, "quick question," or noticed how your grocery cart mysteriously filled with carbs and cleaning supplies, the universal signs of a person holding it together by interpretive dance. None of that disappears just because there are still a few places where you hesitate. That's being human, not behind.

It's not unkind. It's just tired of watching you rehearse a life you're clearly meant to live for real.

By the time this month arrives, you usually know what needs to happen. Maybe you've known for months and were hoping the universe would issue a formal announcement or at least send a sign with better handwriting. But Fire Horse years aren't built on permission slips. They're built on the simple truth that most people are far more capable than their fear would like to admit.

So March steps in with a very reasonable proposition:

What if you just take the step that's been haunting you, and see what happens?

Not a leap. Not a reinvention. Not a public declaration that makes everyone on social media applaud. Just the next thing—the thing that's been following you around like an unpaid intern waiting for instructions.

You don't need bravery in its movielike form. You need the form of courage that looks almost boring from the outside: telling the truth, choosing the obvious thing, and moving toward what's been calling your name long before you felt "ready."

March doesn't care about readiness. March cares about honesty—and the grounded optimism that unfolds when you stop outsmarting your own direction and finally walk toward it.

Prompts for March

1. **What decision have you already made internally, despite pretending you're still "thinking it over"?**
   You know the one.
2. **Where are you mistaking fear for logic?**
   Fear loves a spreadsheet. Don't be fooled.
3. **What would you choose if you weren't trying to be impressive, strategic, or universally admired?**
   Practical honesty over performance.
4. **Where is life nudging you in the same direction over and over again, as if it's tired of repeating itself?**
   Patterns are messages. Notice them.
5. **What's one step—embarrassingly small, almost underwhelming—that would prove you're actually moving?**
   Momentum doesn't need applause. Just motion.

Practice for March

A Practice in Removing the Middleman (i.e., Fear)

Identify one action you've been postponing because you insist on "getting everything in order first."

Spoiler: nothing will ever be in perfect order. Start anyway.

Now reduce that action to the smallest non-ridiculous version possible. Not glamorous. Not optimized. But real.

Do that version. Not tomorrow. Not when Mercury behaves. Today.

Then reflect—not as a performance review of your soul —on three things:

1. What felt lighter?
2. What felt inconvenient but survivable?
3. What felt like relief disguised as effort?

You're not building discipline for its own sake. You're building a life that doesn't fold every time fear clears its throat.

APRIL — STANDING WHERE YOUR LIFE ACTUALLY IS

By April, the performance pressure of the new year has mostly died down. The motivational noise has retreated back to whatever corner of the internet it crawled out of, and you're left with something far more useful: the truth of your actual life. Not the aspirational version. Not the "On Monday I'll be a new person" version. The real, lived, imperfect, fully human version.

And here's the thing—April isn't asking you to reinvent that life. It's asking you to **step into it.**

In a Fire Horse year, this month carries the energy of coherence—not the glamorous kind, the functional kind. Here, your inner compass starts pointing in a direction that makes sense for reasons you can't always articulate but absolutely feel. You may find, unsurprisingly, that your patience for nonsense remains exactly as low as it's been. The difference now is that you no longer feel obligated to make excuses for it. What restores you stays. What drains you does not. It's less a transformation and more a continued refusal to serve as anyone's unpaid emotional intern in a group project you never volunteered for.

April is where internal truth starts leaking into your external choices. Not as a dramatic transformation montage—but as a shift in how you inhabit your own story. You may find yourself reaching for routines, relationships, or ideas that feel like home, and backing away from the ones that feel like you've been auditioning for a role you don't want.

This month asks one simple, irritatingly honest question: **Are you standing inside your life or just hovering near the doorway?**

Because the doorway is familiar, but it doesn't move you forward.

Standing inside your life looks like letting your daily decisions reflect what your internal life has been whispering (or yelling) for months. It looks like giving weight to what feels real to you—not what has been marketed to you. It looks like being present enough to notice when something fits, and brave enough to admit when it doesn't.

Let April be the month you stop skimming the surface of yourself. Stand where you are, fully. Stand where you're going, with your eyes open. And notice the surprising steadiness that arrives when your inner life and outer life stop contradicting each other.

Prompts for April

1. What feels more aligned now than it did three months ago—and what subtly shifted to make that possible?
Look for the evidence of your own evolution, not the fireworks.

2. Where are you still minimizing, apologizing, or negotiating your truth?
And what would it look like to simply…stop?

3. What story, expectation, or responsibility no longer matches the person you're becoming?
Accuracy is not betrayal.

4. Which decision feels right in your body, even if your mind is drafting a dissertation on why it's "not the right time"?
Your body often knows before your courage catches up.

5. What part of your life is asking you to step in with both feet instead of just dipping a toe?
Half-presence creates half-results. Name where you want to be whole.

Practice for April

A Practice of Occupying Your Actual Life

Choose one area where you've been under-participating —a boundary you keep softening, a desire you keep postponing, a responsibility you half-do out of habit, a version of yourself you only inhabit on good days.

For one month, commit to showing up for *just that one area* with full presence:
Not perfection.
Not martyrdom.
Not a brand-new identity.
Just presence.

Each week, ask: **Am I standing inside this part of my life, or am I standing beside it?**

Note what changes when you begin acting from alignment rather than obligation. Note who responds well—and who only liked you half-present because it benefited them. Note the steadiness that forms when your choices finally match your knowing.

You're not trying to impress anyone. You're trying to be congruent—and your future self will thank you for the accuracy.

MAY — THE LINE YOU (HOPEFULLY) STOP MOVING

By May, the universe stops entertaining your internal monologues about "soon." The incremental shifts you've been making—the boundaries you set, the patterns you interrupted, the truths you accidentally admitted on a Tuesday—start arranging themselves into something annoyingly clear: you're moving forward whether you feel poetic about it or not.

In a Fire Horse year, May is where movement stops being theoretical.

All the things you said you *might* do, *should* do, *will definitely start next week* begin tapping their foot. Not out of impatience—out of recognition. You've done enough sorting and circling. Something in you knows what it's time to choose, even if you haven't written it neatly in your planner (which you bought specifically for this purpose and barely use).

This isn't reinvention. It's reinforcement. It's the month where your life quietly mutters, *"Okay, but seriously—are we doing this or not?"*

And for once…you might actually answer it.

Momentum in May doesn't care about speed. It cares about accuracy. It shows up in the moments where things feel slightly less impossible, where a bit of ease slips in without asking permission, where you find yourself reaching for choices you used to avoid because you were too tired, too scared, or too busy being responsible for everyone else's comfort.

This is the month where you stop talking yourself out of the life that keeps trying to choose you.

Let May be the month you commit to the direction that already has your pull—the one that feels like relief, not performance. Leaning is still movement. And this month, leaning counts.

Prompts for May

1. **Where are you already experiencing movement —even if it's inconsistent, messy, or slightly embarrassing?**
   Momentum rarely looks inspirational at first.
2. **What feels easier now than it did in January—and what does that ease reveal about where you actually belong?**
   Ease is a compass, not a coincidence.
3. **What are you finally done pretending you don't want?**
   Be honest. It's May. The performance contract expired.

4. **Where do you feel a forward pull—not pressure, not obligation, but possibility?**
   Follow the direction that feels like oxygen.
5. **What's one small, repeatable action that would actually support your growth instead of sabotaging it?**
   Think sustainable. Not cinematic.

Practice for May

A Practice of Calling Your Own Bluff

Choose one area of your life where you've already made progress—however small—and stop acting like it was an accident.

Then reinforce it with a single weekly action. Not a life overhaul, not an aggressive new routine—a realistic, adult decision that says:

"Yes, I'm taking myself seriously now."

At the end of the month, review what strengthened, what stabilized, and what finally stopped requiring pep talks. Momentum grows when you stop negotiating with what's already working.

JUNE — LETTING YOURSELF BE HELPED (ON PURPOSE, NOT ACCIDENTALLY)

There comes a point in every year—and in every life— when your capacity stops pretending it's limitless. June sits right at that intersection. The midpoint. The reality check. The moment you discover that "pushing through" is no longer a personality trait so much as a warning sign.

For many people—especially those raised to be the reliable one, the strong one, the translator, the fixer, the emotional shock-absorber—asking for help was never framed as a reasonable option. You learned to solve, soothe, shoulder, and smile. The requests you never made still live in your body. The support you didn't get still shapes how you breathe.

And yet here you are—in a month that finally calls your bluff.

Not by shaming your self-sufficiency, and certainly not by insisting you "just open up" (nothing is more irritating). June simply lifts a mirror you can no longer dodge: **carrying everything alone is not strength; it's self-erasure dressed as competence.**

Because for many of us, "competence" has really meant this: *erase yourself fast enough that no one notices you needed anything in the first place.* It's vanishing in plain sight. It's becoming the person everyone relies on because you've trained them—without realizing it—to expect you to have no limits. Efficient, yes. Sustainable? Absolutely not.

Fire Horse energy in June is firm but fair. It doesn't nudge you toward dependence; it nudges you toward honesty. It reminds you that sovereignty is not isolation —it's discernment. You get to decide who has earned the right to stand beside you. You get to choose what support looks like. You get to stop entertaining people who think "checking in" is an Olympic sport.

This month is about practicing the radical, deeply uncomfortable truth that letting yourself be accompanied is not a sign of weakness—it's a sign you plan to survive in something resembling wholeness.

June invites you to recognize your limits without shame, your needs without apology, and your desire for connection without branding it as failure.

And maybe—if the conditions are right—you let one good, consistent person get close enough to matter.

Prompts for June

Write or speak—whichever gets you closer to honesty:

1. **Where have you confused endurance with strength, and what has that confusion cost you?**
   Even five percent less self-abandonment is progress.
2. **Who in your life has repeatedly shown up without asking you to shrink, translate, or pretend?**
   Name what makes that possible.
3. **What support do you need that you've never said out loud—and what is the smallest, safest version of naming it?**
   Small truths count.
4. **What becomes visible when you stop performing capacity you do not have?**
   Visibility is not the same as vulnerability.
5. **Where have you been loyal to exhaustion, and what new loyalty might serve you better?**
   Choose yourself without ceremony.

Practice for June

The One Ask Ritual

Choose **one** thing—small, specific, and human—and ask someone you trust for it.

Not a grand gesture. Not an emotional audit. Not a secret test disguised as an errand.

Something like:

"Can you walk with me while I talk this out?"
"Would you check in with me this week?"
"Could you help me decide between two options?"

The point is not whether the person says yes. The point is teaching your nervous system that reaching out is not a catastrophe. That connection doesn't detonate your life. That you don't have to cosplay invincibility to be loved, respected, or taken seriously.

June is the month you let someone shoulder one corner of the weight—not to weaken you, but to widen your life.

JULY — THE QUIET BRAVERY OF NOT BOLTING

Some forms of courage will never trend, sell out stadiums, or be adapted into prestige television. July deals in a different kind of bravery—the bravery you practice in your own kitchen, on your commute, in the mirror, or in the moments when no one is watching but you. It's the courage of staying with yourself instead of sprinting toward the nearest distraction simply because discomfort knocked.

By midyear, old patterns love to make a cameo. Doubt returns with the confidence of a former tenant. Habits you swore you deleted start rattling the doorknob. The world, for its part, continues demanding that you be competent, accommodating, unbothered, available, resilient, and, ideally, undemanding. But a Fire Horse year does not reward disappearing acts. It rewards people who stop abandoning themselves.

July asks you to remain present in the room of your own life long enough to tell the truth inside it—not the polished version, not the PR-friendly one, but the honest one that doesn't care about optics. This isn't about improvement. It's about recognition. It's about refusing to treat your own needs like an inconvenience. It's about acknowledging the pattern you're done explaining away, the boundary you're done negotiating, the truth you're done dodging.

Call it what you want. July asks you to stay.

This month poses three questions that won't flatter you, but will free you:

- **Where do you stand with yourself when pressure rises?**
- **What truth is tapping its foot impatiently, waiting for you to stop looking away?**
- **What direction feels honest—not impressive, not efficient, *honest*?**

You don't need fireworks to be brave. You need presence, patience, and the willingness to stop fleeing your own life.

Prompts for July

1. **Where do you tend to "leave yourself" when discomfort hits—overworking, care-taking, disappearing, numbing, charming, performing?**
   Not to criticize the pattern. Only to identify the exit door you use most often.
2. **What truth keeps circling back no matter how many times you try to outrun it?**

If it keeps returning, it's not noise—it's instruction.

3. **What is one small, exact act of courage that would bring your inner life and outer choices into closer alignment?**
   Courage isn't volume. It's accuracy.
4. **What pressure are you carrying that never belonged to you in the first place—and who taught you to carry it?**
   Returning the weight is its own act of bravery.
5. **Where is the line between responsibility and self-erasure in your life right now?**
   Locate the edge where care becomes cost.

Practice for July

The Courage Inventory

Choose one day this month and move at half your normal speed. Nothing mystical. Nothing "ritualized." Just slower. (No soundtrack required.)

Throughout the day, notice each moment when your instinct is to:

- rush past a feeling,
- downplay a need,
- soften a truth,
- or perform a version of yourself that no longer fits.

Each time you catch yourself doing it—pause. One breath. Tell yourself: **I don't leave myself here.**

That night, write down *three* moments when you stayed. Not perfectly. Just honestly.

This is the integrity that changes a life—the integrity of not abandoning yourself at the very moment you need your own presence the most.

AUGUST — THE POLITE REFUSAL TO LOSE YOURSELF

August doesn't arrive gently. It shows up like the friend who walks into your apartment, looks around, and says, "So…we're still doing *this*?" Not rudely—just observantly. Because by August, the year has collected enough evidence to form an opinion, and honestly, so have you.

The heat alone strips away pretense. You can't lie to yourself when you're this tired, this sun-wilted, this done with everyone's unnecessary drama. What you tolerate becomes embarrassingly obvious. What you avoid becomes loud. What you've been negotiating with yourself all summer? Suddenly looks like a bad deal you signed under emotional duress.

August isn't here to scold you. It's here to simplify you. To nudge you toward honesty the same way humidity nudges your hair toward volume—unavoidably, and with zero concern for your aesthetic preferences.

This is the month you stop offering customer service energy to situations that don't deserve it. The month you retract your availability from anything that drains you. The month you realize that "being reasonable" has usually meant silencing your instincts, smoothing over other people's discomfort, carrying the weight of their expectations without complaint, and shrinking yourself just enough to remain "palatable" to people who rely on your strength but resent your boundaries.

And August…well, August is allergic to disappearing.

It won't demand a grand declaration. It just asks one clarifying question: **What are you staying for?**

And if the answer is obligation, habit, guilt, or "I already paid the annual fee," then congratulations—you've found the exact place where your self-respect wants to stretch.

Reflection Prompts for August

Where in your life do you feel most like yourself—the version who doesn't rehearse?
If the only place is "alone in my car," take that seriously.

1. **What are you staying for—truly?**
   Habit is not a reason; it's a reflex.
2. **Which patterns keep luring you back into versions of yourself you're trying to outgrow?**
   Patterns are persistent. Good thing you're stubborn.

3. **Which truths have been politely tapping all year while you pretended you didn't hear them?**
   They're not going away.
4. **Where would one simple boundary save you hours of emotional cleanup?**
   Efficiency is spiritual too.

Practice for August

The Line You Step Back Into (Without Apology)

Choose one area of your life where your needs have been treated like an optional subscription—renewable only when convenient to others.

Write one sentence naming *what you actually need* there. Make it honest. Make it simple. Make it yours.

Read it once a day for a week. Not as an affirmation. Not as a prophecy. Just as a reminder that your needs are not negotiable fine print.

Soft assertion isn't loud. It's **consistent**—and consistency is where self-respect learns to live.

SEPTEMBER — WHEN THE MATH STARTS MATHING

By September, the year stops flirting and starts telling the truth. Not gently, not cruelly—just plainly. September is that friend who loves you enough to say, "Okay, but what are we *actually* doing?" while handing you a glass of water because you clearly haven't hydrated since March.

This is the point when all the bright, ambitious January fantasies meet the lived reality of your bandwidth, your boundaries, and the ongoing circus of being a person. The Fire Horse year doesn't judge—but it does keep receipts. And by September, the math starts mathing.

Here's the gift, though:

September is not here to expose you. It's here to **relieve** you. There is nothing more exhausting than pretending a goal still matters when you've secretly broken up with it. There is nothing more liberating than admitting that something you've been dragging behind you lost its relevance six months ago. Honesty is not always glamorous, but it is wildly efficient.

And because we are telling the truth:

September isn't scolding you for what didn't bloom. It's helping you notice what *survived* anyway—what still has pulse, purpose, and potential if you'd stop downplaying it like it's a side hobby and not the thing that keeps tapping you on the shoulder.

For many women—and especially for Black women— September lands with a particular charge. We know what it means for a year to "take time" we were never actually given.

We know how often "be reasonable" shows up as its real cousins:
"You're too direct,"
"Maybe soften your delivery,"
"Don't take it personally,"
"Don't make this a thing,"
"Be grateful,"
"Stop overthinking it,"
"You're being aggressive,"
"Keep the peace,"
"You're asking for too much,"
"That's just how things are,"
"Maybe you misinterpreted,"
"You'll get your chance,"
or the elite favorite—"Can we circle back to that?"
which is corporate for: *bury it and never speak of it again.*

Black women hear the advanced settings of these messages—the ones disguised as advice, professionalism, humility, or sacrifice.

September does not entertain any of that. September says:

“If you were waiting for permission to choose a life that fits you—surprise. You’re the committee.”

This is the month that asks the deceptively simple question: **What’s still worth your effort—and what isn’t worth another ounce of your spirit?**

Not a breakdown. Not a sweeping overhaul. Just the steadiness that settles the ground beneath you and shows you where your next step actually is.

A shift toward the truth you’ve been carrying for months.

If January made promises and June illuminated the truth, September stands at the doorway with a raised eyebrow and says, quite reasonably: **“Okay. Now what?”**

Reflection Prompts for September

1. **What has steadily endured this year beneath your doubts, distractions, or chaos?**

Some things persist for a reason. Notice the reason.

2. **Which goals belonged to a past version of you —and why are you still carrying them?**
   Retiring a goal isn't failure. It's administrative self-respect.
3. **Where have you been forcing momentum that never wanted you in the first place?**
   If you're pushing a brick wall, that's not ambition— that's choreography.
4. **What felt meaningful in January that still feels meaningful now?**
   Longevity reveals truth better than enthusiasm ever could.
5. **Which part of your year is tugging gently (or loudly) for a course correction?**
   A shift by two degrees can save an entire trajectory.

Practice for September

The Honest Ledger

Make two columns:

- **What Kept Showing Up**
- **What Only Looked Good on Paper**

Under *What Kept Showing Up*, list what reappeared without force—ideas, desires, insights, people who didn't drain you, truths you tried to ignore.

Under *What Only Looked Good on Paper*, place the things that sounded impressive but never aligned with your real life.

Then circle one item from each. Ask yourself:
What do I need to honor the first?
What do I need to release the second?

Not all progress moves forward. Sometimes progress is simply telling the truth about where you've been standing—and finally choosing a direction that respects your actual life.

OCTOBER — THE CLEARING THAT TELLS THE TRUTH

By October, the year delivers its clearing the way life usually does—bluntly, efficiently, and right on time. Not to punish you, but to spare you one more month of managing what you already know isn't working. There's something about this month that strips the noise from your life and leaves you with what's actually yours. Not what you committed to out of guilt. Not what you performed because it looked good on paper. Not what you inherited from someone else's expectations.

Just **you**, standing in the middle of everything you've agreed to carry.

October has a gift for revealing excess—the emotional clutter, the half-finished obligations, the stories you've been re-running in your head like reruns of a show you don't even like anymore. It's the moment you realize you've been trying to keep too many plates spinning, and some of them aren't even your plates. Some of them aren't even cute.

This month asks a simple, necessary, annoyingly clarifying question:

Do you actually need all this?

Most of us don't. But we cling to it anyway because chaos can feel like evidence that we care, or proof that we're working hard, or a distraction from the truth we're avoiding.

But the Fire Horse year has no patience for ornamental struggle. It's not impressed by busy calendars, emotional acrobatics, or the illusion of productivity. It cares about **trajectory**, not accumulation. So October becomes the month where you practice letting go in ways that don't look glamorous, but feels like oxygen.

Not a purge. Not a performance. Just the grown-up decision to stop giving every passing thought, task, and person unrestricted access to your energy like it's a public utility.

What stays is what steadies you. What goes is anything that keeps you bargaining with your own peace.

It doesn't need to be philosophical. It doesn't need to be deep. It just has to be honest enough that *you* recognize yourself in it.

Reflection Prompts for October

1. **What part of your life feels overcrowded—mentally, emotionally, or spiritually?**
   Where do you feel the "too much" most clearly in your body?
2. **What are you still maintaining out of habit rather than alignment?**
   Not the stuff you dislike—the stuff you've already outgrown.
3. **Whose expectations are you unconsciously carrying?**
   And what becomes possible when you set them down?
4. **What truth have you avoided because naming it would require a shift?**
   You don't have to act on it. Just tell the truth.
5. **What becomes simpler—and truer—when you choose what strengthens you over what impresses anyone else?**

Practice for October

The Life Edit (One Honest Corner at a Time)

Choose **one tiny area** of your life to clear out:
A drawer.
A note folder.
An email thread.
A sentence you keep repeating that no longer fits.
A commitment you said yes to out of politeness, not desire.

The point isn't the item. It's the **signal** you send yourself when you remove something that has outlived its usefulness.

As you release it, say: **"Thank you for what you were. You don't have to take space from me anymore."**

Notice what settles in the space that remains. That lightness—that steadying—is the real harvest of October.

THE SEASON THAT TELLS ON US

There's a particular kind of pressure that arrives this time of year—a cultural cocktail mixed from nostalgia, marketing campaigns, family expectations, and whatever capitalism managed to convince you is "essential" to belonging. The holidays have a way of magnifying everything: the joy, the grief, the gaps, the growth, the parts of your life that feel abundant, and the parts that feel like they need a structural engineer.

It's not just about consumerism—though the world will absolutely try to sell you the illusion that buying something is the same as becoming someone. It's the emotional choreography we're all expected to perform. The smiling, the gathering, the pretending those dynamics don't unravel you from the inside out. The pressure to be grateful, sentimental, available, and stable all at once, as if any of us have ever existed with that level of emotional multitasking.

And for many people—especially those carrying intergenerational roles, cultural expectations, caretaking responsibilities, or the unspoken job of "keeping everything from falling apart." The holiday season isn't a break; it's a workload. A cumulative intensification. A stretch of weeks where the gap between who you're told to be and who you actually are widens just enough to become impossible to ignore.

This section of the book doesn't pretend the season is gentle. It doesn't assume December brings resolution wrapped in twinkle lights. It doesn't romanticize resilience or prescribe joy like a vitamin.

Instead, it offers a new approach: moving through the final months with honesty, not performance. With awareness instead of obligation. With a grounded sense of self that does not evaporate just because the calendar says it's time to host, gather, give, or endure.

This is where the work of the Fire Horse year becomes unmistakably practical.

The holiday season exposes the truths we've been negotiating all year—what drains us, what sustains us, what roles we inherited rather than chose, and what boundaries we've been afraid to name.

It forces the question:

How do I stay inside my life without disappearing into everyone else's needs?

As you enter November and December, this book isn't asking you to become festive. It's inviting you to remain *real*. To let the season reveal what has shifted within you. To notice where your energy contracts or expands. To honor the truths you've gathered, the losses you've carried, the growth you've earned, and the unseen progress no one else witnessed.

Navigating these months is not about performing holiday spirit. It's about learning to belong to yourself in a season that often demands the opposite. And for those who *love* this time of year—the lights, the meals, the gatherings, the excuse to decorate something within an inch of its life—there is room for that, too. Joy doesn't make you naïve. Delight doesn't make you unserious. Sometimes the cooler air, the color shift, or the ritual of dusting off the one playlist that *always* hits can steady you in ways the rest of the year couldn't manage.

Whether this season overwhelms you or energizes you—whether it asks more of you or somehow returns you to yourself—the invitation is the same: move through it on your terms. Not out of habit. Not out of obligation. Not out of pressure to match anyone else's emotional temperature.

Belong to yourself, even here. Especially here.

And that—without ceremony—is liberation.

NOVEMBER — THE YEAR IN ITS REAL CLOTHES

By November, the year drops the act.

The pep talk of January is a distant memory, the productive delusion of spring has expired, and even summer's bravado has stopped pretending it can carry you the rest of the way. What you're left with is whatever managed to withstand your moods, your doubt, your schedule, your avoidance, your growth, and your very human attempts to run from the truth.

In other words: the real stuff.

November doesn't arrive with drama. It arrives with accuracy. It's the month where you finally see what's been holding steady—not because you clung to it, but because it never required performance to exist. Everything else? It starts slipping without ceremony out of your hands, mostly because you're too tired to keep forcing what never fit in the first place.

And here's the part people don't talk about: honesty is exhausting before it's liberating.

When the noise of the year fades, the honest signal comes through—and sometimes that signal is comforting, and sometimes it's the emotional equivalent of finding out the warranty is expired. But either way, it tells the truth. And truth, even when inconvenient, is merciful.

This is the month that asks a gentler but more pointed question:

After everything—the progress, the detours, the surprises, the disappointments, the small miracles—what remains true about you?

Not the aspirational version. Not the curated version. Not the "if everything goes right" version. Just the truth your life keeps repeating when you're too tired to interrupt it.

In a Fire Horse year—a year that is allergic to pretense and deeply loyal to direction—November becomes the hinge between who you've been and who you're capable of being. Not transformative through force, but through refusal—refusal to override what you already know, refusal to contort yourself back into shapes you've outgrown, refusal to pretend the year didn't teach you what it taught you.

November isn't asking for reinvention. It's asking for recognition.

What wouldn't leave.
What couldn't last.
And the strength you spent getting here, even if no one clapped for it.

This is the month you stop negotiating with what you already know.

Reflection Prompts for November—The Unavoidable Truths

1. What truth about yourself or your life has repeated all year long, no matter how many times you tried to reroute it?
(Write it plainly. No metaphors. No cushioning.)

2. What have you been carrying that no longer supports you?
(Is it weight, or is it support? Be honest.)

3. Where did you surprise yourself—positively or painfully—and what does that reveal about what's actually true now?

4. What belief about yourself feels outdated, like a file you forgot to delete?
(It doesn't need judgment. Just closure.)

5. If nothing around you changed—not the people, not the deadlines, not the circumstances—what

inner shift would still bring you relief?
(Name the shift, then name the cost of avoiding it.)

Practice for November — The True List

Set a timer for ten minutes.

At the top of the page (or in your journal write):

What I Know Now

Let your hand move. No editing, no performing, no "making it make sense." Write truths—the quiet ones, the loud ones, the reluctant ones, the ones you wish weren't true but keep resurfacing anyway.

When the timer ends, underline **three statements** that feel non-negotiable. These aren't goals. They aren't resolutions. They're coordinates. Let them lead you through the last stretch of the year. December is coming —and December listens to whatever truth you decide to stand with.

DECEMBER — AFTER ALL THAT

By December, the year has stopped performing. So have most people.

There's a particular honesty that arrives when you've made it through twelve months of trying, adjusting, renegotiating, and occasionally sprinting toward things you didn't even want. The beauty of this month is that it doesn't ask you to recap anything, redeem anything, or transform anything into a lesson. It simply invites you to notice what's left standing after everything else has had its say.

December is not sentimental. It isn't here to impress you. It isn't staging a finale or pretending the year has been a neatly written story. It's the month that looks you straight in the eye and says, **"After all that...what now?"**

There's humor in it, if you squint—humor that comes from realizing how much time we spend trying to manage our lives into submission, only to discover that life was never waiting on our perfection. It's been waiting on our participation.

December asks for something different than ambition:
It asks for accuracy. Not who you wanted to be this year, but who you actually became. Not the story you rehearsed, but the one you lived.

And because this is a Fire Horse year, the question beneath every question becomes louder here: **What direction feels honest now?**

Not impressive.
Not efficient.
Not molded for public consumption.
Honest.

This month clarifies what survived your doubts, your distractions, your detours, your breakthroughs, your almosts, your endings, your beginnings, and the handful of days you barely got through. What remains is rarely glamorous—often it's a truth you circled for months, a need you finally admitted, or a desire you can no longer pretend is negotiable.

December isn't here to judge the year. It's here to distill it. To strip the narrative down to its bones so you can see, without theatrics, what matters enough to carry forward—and what can be retired without ceremony.

There is a particular integrity in this way of seeing. Not the fireworks version. The grounded one—where you finally give yourself permission to let the year be exactly what it was, not the version you wished it had been.

And once you stop arguing with reality, you can start shaping what comes next.

After all that…you're still here. And that counts for more than most people are willing to admit.

Reflection Prompts for December

1. **What part of this year revealed something true about you that you can't ignore anymore?**
   Call it what it is.
2. **What did you stop pretending about—deliberately or accidentally?**
   What relief did it bring?
3. **What stayed steady even when you didn't?**
   What does that say about where your life wants to go?
4. **Which desire, boundary, or truth did you meet this year that feels non-negotiable now?**
   Name it plainly.
5. **If you carried only three lessons—the real kind, not the decorative kind—into the next year, what would they be?**

Practice for December

The Three Lines That Matter

On a blank page, write three lines only:

What I Know Now:
What I'm Done Carrying:
What I'm Choosing Next:

Under each heading, write **one sentence**—short, plain, and honest. Do not explain, elaborate, or justify. The point isn't detail. The point is direction. Just the truth in its most unedited form.

Fold the page and place it inside the journal. Read it on the first day of the new year. Adjust nothing. Trust what you wrote when the year was honest with you.

Quarterly Check-Ins

Q1 CHECK-IN — CLARITY

(January • February • March)

The first months of any year hold more questions than answers. You may have moved slowly, or boldly, or inconsistently. It doesn't matter. What matters is noticing what has begun to take shape beneath the surface. Clarity rarely arrives all at once. It comes in pieces—a sentence you keep repeating, a frustration you can't ignore, a desire that keeps tugging at you even when you try to set it aside.

This check-in isn't about measuring your progress. It's about acknowledging what has already begun.

Reflection Prompts

1. What feels clearer now than it did in January, even if you didn't act on it yet?
2. What truth has been following you through these months?
3. Which part of you is asking to be taken more seriously?

Practice

Write down one insight from Q1 that deserves attention. Let that truth shape your next step—not your whole year, just the next step.

Q2 CHECK-IN — DIRECTION

(April • May • June)

By midyear, the path you're walking becomes easier to see. Maybe not the whole thing—but enough to choose where your energy goes and where it no longer belongs. This is the season of course-correction, not self-criticism. A season to ask whether your choices reflect the life you say you want, or the life you've outgrown.

Direction is not about speed. It's about alignment. Where you aim determines where you arrive.

Reflection Prompts

1. What decisions this quarter felt aligned—even if they were uncomfortable?
2. Where have you been drifting when you meant to be choosing?
3. What direction feels honest, even if it scares you?

Practice

Choose one area of your life to realign. Make the adjustment small but deliberate—a shift in routine, a boundary, a clarified commitment.

Q3 CHECK-IN — RENEWAL

(July • August • September)

This is the stretch where the year begins to feel long. Your energy may dip, your expectations may shift, and things you thought were settled may look different now. Renewal is not about reinvention; it's about returning to yourself with compassion. It's the reminder that progress is uneven, and growth often happens beneath the surface long before you see proof.

This check-in is your permission to breathe, reassess, and gather what you need for the months ahead.

Reflection Prompts

1. Where do you feel worn thin, and what would it look like to rest without guilt?
2. What part of your life needs refreshing—not erasing, just tending?
3. What have you learned about your resilience this year?

Practice

Remove one unnecessary pressure from your life for the next seven days. Replace it with something that restores you — rest, connection, or silence.

Q4 CHECK-IN — INTEGRATION

(October • November • December)

The final months of the year call you inward. Not to judge yourself, but to gather the pieces of who you've become. Integration is the quiet work of recognizing your growth and understanding how it lives in your body, your choices, your relationships, your sense of self. It's where everything you've learned begins to find its place.

You don't need to have a perfect ending. You just need an honest one.

Reflection Prompts

1. What lessons from this year have taken root in you?
2. How has your understanding of yourself shifted —subtly or significantly?
3. What feels complete, and what feels ready to continue into the next year?

Practice

Write a brief reflection—no more than a page—describing who you are at this moment. Not who you were. Not who you hope to be. Who you are now. This is your anchor for the next beginning.

Closing Manifesto — For the Year You Choose Yourself

If you've stayed with this work until now, then something in it met you where you were. That matters. Not because this book transformed you overnight, but because you were willing to look at yourself without flinching. You were willing to pause long enough to notice what you've been carrying and what you no longer want to.

This year has not been simple. It asked things of you. It asked for patience you didn't always have and honesty you might have postponed in other seasons. It asked you to examine decisions you once made for survival and consider whether they still fit. You showed up anyway. Not perfectly. Not every day. But often enough to recognize what was true.

There are parts of this year you may not miss. The uncertainty. The tension. The conversations that left you quieter than you expected. The moments when clarity cost you comfort. And still, there is something here worth keeping. A steadier understanding of yourself. A clearer sense of where your limits are. A deeper awareness of what you will no longer negotiate.

That kind of clarity doesn't arrive in dramatic declarations. It builds slowly. In the decisions you made when no one was watching. In the boundaries you held without announcement. In the quiet refusals that didn't need to be explained. In the private admissions you allowed onto the page.

If you feel different now, that isn't accidental. You have been paying attention. And attention changes people. It rearranges priorities. It softens what used to feel urgent. It strengthens what used to feel fragile. It makes it harder to participate in versions of yourself that no longer feel honest.

Choosing yourself is not a performance. It is not a public declaration. It is a series of internal alignments. It is recognizing when you are about to abandon your own knowing and deciding not to. It is letting your limits stand without apology. It is allowing your life to reflect who you are now, not who you had to be to endure.

You do not need to prove this shift to anyone. You do not need to dramatize it. Just notice what feels more solid than it did before. Notice what no longer requires explanation. Notice where you have stopped arguing with yourself.

As this chapter closes, there is no ceremony required. Just a quiet acknowledgment that you walked through something and came out more aligned with yourself than when you began. That is what it means to choose yourself in a year that demanded clarity.

That's the work.

— Tasha

The Fire Horse Reciprocity Principles — How We Stay Standing

Community is not a buzzword. It's an ecosystem—a rhythm of give and receive, a balance of being held and holding others without losing yourself in the exchange. If the past few years revealed anything, it's that the myth of self-sufficiency isn't noble. It's a slow collapse in disguise. People who try to carry everything alone don't become stronger; they just become harder to see until they break in places no one notices.

Reciprocity is not networking. It is not performance. It is not matching energies like you're settling a bill.

Reciprocity is simply **the practice of showing up for yourself the same way you value the people who show up for you.**

And in a Fire Horse year—a year that demands honesty in motion—reciprocity becomes a discipline rooted in intention, not obligation.

The Principles:

1. Give only what you can offer with integrity.

Not everything. Not endlessly. Not to prove you're worthy. Just what's real—the measure of offering that doesn't deplete you or distort you.

2. Receive without apology or theatrics.

Let people care for you without turning it into a performance review. Let yourself be seen without sprinting to dim the light.

3. Build connections that don't require an audition.

Belonging should not cost you your self-respect, your boundaries, or your bandwidth. If you have to shrink to fit, it's not reciprocity—it's erosion.

4. Practice accountability that feels like care, not surveillance.

Accountability isn't punishment. It's the courage to tell the truth in relationships that can actually withstand it.

5. Choose community that honors your humanity —not your highlight reel.

The real you deserves room to breathe. The people meant for you won't require a curated version.

Reciprocity is the infrastructure of resilience. It's how we stay upright in a world that pulls us in every direction. It's how we prevent ourselves—and each other—from slipping through cracks we were never meant to navigate alone.

This principle is not soft. It's foundational. It's how you build a life that can hold you—and a circle that can sustain you—without requiring your constant self-abandonment.

Building Your Circle With Intention

Long before we had language for "boundaries" or "healthy relationships," people gathered in circles. Not because it was symbolic. Because it worked.

Circles kept people close enough to protect one another without trapping anyone. Everyone could be seen. Everyone could listen. No one was pushed to the edges where resentment or quiet power could build unnoticed.

Families sat this way. Councils met this way. Grief, celebration, decision, repair—all of it happened in the round. Even early shelters were shaped this way. And when someone was pushed outside that shape, the meaning was clear. You were no longer inside the protection.

We like to think we've outgrown that logic. That adulthood is more advanced now. That community can be assembled through proximity, shared calendars, or an algorithm that suggests people who like the same things we do.

But the truth hasn't changed much.

Your life is still shaped by who stands closest to you and who you allow to stay there. Not in theory. In practice.

Over time, patterns reveal themselves. Who steadies you. Who leaves you wrung out. Who listens without trying to correct you. Who keeps asking you to explain yourself until you forget what you were trying to say in the first place.

Who treats access to you as care. And who treats it as entitlement.

This year, especially, asks for clarity about proximity. Not perfection. Clarity. Because most of us inherited circles drawn out of habit, obligation or survival. They were built to get us through something, not necessarily to support the lives we're living now.

This section isn't about labeling people as "good" or "bad." It's about noticing the structure you're already inside. Who is close. Who is distant. Who has remained near simply because no one ever questioned it.

From there, the work becomes practical, not dramatic.

You begin to see who actually supports you. Who functions better with some distance. Who you've been carrying beyond what the relationship was built to hold.

Not as a judgment. As information.

Before the circle changes, you have to see the landscape clearly.

Not everyone in your life belongs at the same distance from your inner world. That isn't a flaw in your character. It's how relationships work.

There's a difference between the people you work with, the people who raised you, the people who know your history, the people who know how you actually live, and the people who can sit with the truth of you without trying to reshape it. Each relationship has a role. Each has limits.

An intentional circle isn't a ranking system. It's about access.

It asks a simple question: who can meet you where you are without asking you to perform, edit or disappear?

Some people remain important but need more distance to stay healthy. Some belong close for a season, not a lifetime. Some drift outward without conflict once you stop forcing the fit.

This isn't about loss. It's about seeing clearly.

You're not building this circle to replace every other relationship in your life. You're building it so you can stay oriented within them. So you're no longer guessing where you stand or what's being asked of you.

An inner circle should bring truth. Not comfort. Not constant agreement. Truth.

What an Intentional Circle Actually Requires

A steady circle isn't built through hope alone or the belief that everyone will eventually show up differently.

It requires three things, in human measure: clarity about how your relationships actually affect you, reciprocity that doesn't have to be negotiated every time, and the willingness to stop explaining away what continues to cost you.

This isn't about emotional polish. It's about attention.

When a relationship consistently leaves you depleted, that matters. When you keep adjusting yourself to maintain peace, that matters. When care flows in only one direction, that matters.

None of that makes you cruel. It makes you honest.

What follows isn't a test. It's a way of seeing what is already true.

Reflection: The Circle You're Living In

Who feels easier to be around—not because they ask nothing of you, but because they don't ask you to vanish?

Who knows the unpolished version of you and doesn't rush to tidy it?

Who leaves you tired even as you keep saying, "It's fine"?

Who celebrates you without comparison or correction?

Who reaches for you when they need something but rarely when you need rest?

Who have you been carrying long after they learned how to stand?

Where do you overgive, overexplain or stay longer than you want to?

These are not accusations. They are observations.

Practice: The Circle Map

Take a blank page and draw three soft circles.

The Center Circle

In the center, place the people who meet you with steadiness and honesty. You don't brace around them. You don't rehearse.

The Middle Circle

In the middle circle, place people you care about but with limits. The relationship matters, but not every part of you is available there.

The Outer Circle

In the outer circle, place the people you engage with respectfully but without intimacy—colleagues, acquaintances, extended ties.

Place names where they already belong.

Then ask yourself: who might move closer, based on how they actually show up? Who might need more distance, based on how much you've been carrying? Where do you need a boundary rather than a disappearance?

You don't have to rearrange your life today. You just have to see it.

A circle is a shape people return to.

This practice helps you return to yourself.

Finding Your Own Voice

The world asks a lot of us. To keep moving. To respond quickly. To have answers ready. To speak with confidence even when we're still sorting through what we think.. Over time, that pressure doesn't just exhaust us. It makes it harder to tell what's actually coming from us and what's coming from outside expectations.

If your voice feels harder to locate than it once did, that isn't a failure of strength or awareness. It's what happens when you've been carrying responsibility for a long time. When you've been responding instead of choosing. When staying functional felt more urgent than checking in with yourself.

Most people don't drift from themselves because they're careless. They drift because they've been prioritizing stability—keeping families, jobs, and expectations from falling apart—over listening to themselves.

At some point, it becomes harder to pretend you don't notice. Not in a dramatic, everything-falls-apart way.

Just in a quiet, steady one. You start to see that the life you've built no longer fits the person you're becoming.

That realization can feel disorienting. You might question yourself. You might wonder if you've made a wrong turn somewhere. It can carry a kind of low-grade fear, as if noticing the mismatch means something is broken.

It doesn't.

It means you've changed. And the change has been asking for your attention. That's often where your voice begins to reappear.

Your voice rarely arrives with certainty. It shows up in smaller ways. In the hesitation you keep brushing past. In the answer that feels steady rather than impressive. In the "no" that keeps returning, even after you've talked yourself out of it.

Listening again doesn't mean you have to start over. It requires giving yourself a little space to notice what you've been pushing down just to stay functional.

Trust rebuilds quietly. Through answering a question honestly instead of automatically. Through pausing before agreeing to something that costs more than you want to give. Through deciding not to justify yourself when explanation only pulls you further from what you know.

This year, let your voice take up space in your decisions again. Not to refine it. Not to polish it. Just to hear what it's actually saying.

You might ask yourself: Does this still belong to me? Do I actually want this? What happens if I answer honestly, even if I don't yet know what comes next?

Your voice doesn't need volume to be reliable. It needs consistency. Each time you listen, even briefly, you reduce the quiet harm that comes from talking yourself out of what you know. You stop shaping your life around expectations that were never yours.

Your voice is where your limits begin to make sense. It's where you start to recognize what feels like enough for you. Strengthening it doesn't mean hardening yourself or pulling away from people. It means being honest with yourself first, before you negotiate with anyone else.

Reflection

Where have you been ignoring your own response lately?

What feels true now, even if you're not ready to act on it?

What changes when you stop explaining and simply listen?

Practice

For the next week, try something simple.

Before answering a request, making a decision or agreeing to something, pause. Ask yourself: Is this coming from habit, or from what I actually know?

The pause doesn't need to fix anything. It only needs to interrupt the reflex.

Small interruptions have a way of returning more than they take.

Carrying the Year Forward — Building a Life That Matches Your Truth

You don't move through a year like this and simply slide back into who you were before. Once you've heard yourself clearly, pretending you didn't takes more effort than honesty ever did. And once you've experienced what it feels like to live without constantly adjusting yourself for survival, it becomes harder to romanticize the arrangements that required you to play it small.

This book was never about improving you. It was about helping you recognize the version of you that has been trying to surface all along. The one who learned how to manage, endure and perform when that was necessary, but never lost track of what it cost.

Carrying this year forward isn't about declarations or dramatic shifts. It's about behaving as if you believe what you've learned. About staying aligned with what you now know, even when the world keeps offering easier versions of you to slip back into. Because it will. Old roles will resurface. Familiar expectations will return. Some people may prefer the version of you that required less from them.

What's different now is simple: you know what it feels like not to abandon yourself. Once you've felt that, it becomes harder to justify doing it again.

What comes next won't look impressive. It will look ordinary. Repetition. Small choices made often enough that they begin to shape your days. The moment you don't talk yourself out of what you know. The moment you say no without explaining it into something softer. The moment you stop pretending you're unsure when you're actually weighing the cost.

From the outside, these decisions won't look dramatic. They'll look quiet. They'll look like someone telling the truth without turning it into a performance.

Carrying this year forward also means learning how to read discomfort differently. Not as proof that you failed, but as evidence that something shifted. Boundaries can feel awkward. New choices can unsettle you. Telling the truth can change the tone of a room. None of that automatically means you were wrong. Often it means you chose deliberately instead of reflexively.

What matters now isn't perfection. It's consistency.

You don't need to become someone else. You need to keep choosing in ways that reflect what you've already learned. Clarity isn't permanent. It's something you practice. Especially on days when the old reflexes show up dressed as logic.

A Simple Check-In

This doesn't need to be ceremonial. It's something you can reach for when you feel yourself slipping back into habit, or when something in your day feels slightly off and you can't name why.

Ask yourself:

Where did I tell myself the truth today?
Even a small one counts.

Where did I move away from myself?
Not dramatically. Just the moment you went along instead of speaking.

Where did I talk myself out of what I knew?
Not to judge it. Just to notice what it required and what it cost.

What did I need in that moment that I didn't give myself?
Not the perfect answer. Just the honest one.

Where did I act from habit instead of choice?
The familiar response. The easy agreement. The version of you that keeps things steady.

What small adjustment would make tomorrow feel more accurate?
Not a reinvention. Just a correction.

These questions aren't about optimization. They're about staying in contact with your own life so you don't wake up one day inside something shaped entirely by pressure, repetition or accommodation.

Carrying the year forward isn't about doing more. It's about noticing when you drift and choosing again without turning it into self-punishment. Some days you'll move forward. Some days you'll pause and reset. Both are part of it.

You're not starting over.

You're starting from awareness.

And that changes what's possible, whether anyone else sees it or not.

The Body Is Not a Detour

Working With the Nervous System You Have in a Fire Horse Year

Fire Horse years are often framed as seasons of momentum, courage, and forward motion. They are described as bold and kinetic, full of drive and decisive energy. What those descriptions tend to overlook is that sustained fire requires containment. Without boundaries, fire doesn't illuminate. It consumes.

This section exists to name something plainly: not everybody moves through a year the same way. Some bodies wake up already negotiating. Some live with pain that arrives without warning, fatigue that doesn't respond to motivation, neurological symptoms that distort memory, language, appetite, and rest. When that is your reality, traditional advice about discipline, productivity, or consistency quickly becomes alienating.

This chapter is not an argument for doing less. It is an argument for doing what is actually sustainable.

Living with chronic symptoms forces a different relationship with time, energy, and self-expectation. Weakness, deep fatigue, joint pain that burns or stabs, persistent migraines, prickling sensations through the muscles, appetite loss, brain fog, and fluctuating capacity are not personal failures. They are signals. Ignoring them does not make you stronger. It only makes recovery more expensive.

A Fire Horse year does not ask you to override your body. It asks you to understand it.

Reframing the Work

The most meaningful shift I have made is this: I stopped treating symptoms as interruptions and started treating them as information. That single change altered how I plan, how I rest, how I speak to myself, and how I define progress.

Symptoms tell you when your nervous system is overloaded. They signal when inflammation, stress, or depletion has crossed a threshold. Responding to that information is not weakness. It is intelligence. In practice, that means replacing rigid expectations with adaptive ones. It means building systems that account for variability instead of pretending it doesn't exist.

This section focuses on tools that help reduce strain rather than eliminate symptoms. There are no cures offered here. There are no promises of transformation.

What follows are supports I rely on regularly to stay oriented, functional, and intact.

Reducing Decision Load

Pain and fatigue significantly increase cognitive load. On difficult days, decision-making itself becomes exhausting. One of the most effective ways to conserve energy is to reduce the number of choices you have to make.

I rely on default routines when capacity is low. This includes rotating the same breakfasts, keeping a small set of reliable meals on hand, using a consistent clothing formula, and maintaining a simple daily rhythm rather than an ambitious task list. These decisions are made once, ahead of time, and reused as needed.

This is not about monotony. It is about protecting mental bandwidth so that limited energy is spent where it actually matters.

Regulating in Short Intervals

Traditional advice often emphasizes extended rest or full recovery periods. When the nervous system is already dysregulated, those expectations can feel unreachable. Instead of aiming for complete calm, I focus on short intervals of regulation.

This may look like lying flat for a few minutes with one hand on the chest, using heat where the body feels inflamed or loud, slowing the breath with a longer exhale, or engaging a familiar sensory input such as a scent or texture. The goal is not total relief. The goal is to lower intensity enough to regain footing.

Small reductions in discomfort accumulate. Relief does not need to be dramatic to be meaningful.

Eating for Stability

On symptomatic days, appetite is often inconsistent or absent. This is not a character flaw, and it is not something to correct through pressure or guilt. I prioritize foods that are warm, simple, and easy to digest. I aim for basic nourishment that supports stability rather than performance.

This approach removes the expectation that eating must be optimal or impressive. It reframes food as cooperation with the body rather than another arena for self-discipline.

Tracking Without Obsession

Tracking symptoms can either sharpen understanding or create anxiety. The difference lies in *purpose*. I track patterns to notice correlations, not to control outcomes. Over time, this has helped me identify what exacerbates fatigue, what shortens pain flares, and which times of day are more forgiving.

This information strengthens self-trust. It allows for better planning without creating a fixation on metrics. The purpose is understanding, not surveillance.

Adjusting the Language of Effort

Language shapes endurance. Phrases like "pushing through," "powering past," or "getting back on track" imply that the body is an adversary to be overridden. I no longer use them.

Instead, I ask practical questions. What is available today? What is the least costly way to approach this task? What can be postponed without consequence? These questions do not lower standards. They refine them.

Longevity requires discernment.

Holding the Hard Truth

Living with chronic symptoms often brings grief for a former version of yourself. That grief is legitimate. It deserves acknowledgment, not dismissal. What this year asks, however, is not that you mourn endlessly, but that you stop structuring your life around a version of yourself that no longer exists.

Building a life that does not require self-abandonment is not resignation. It is mastery.

Fire Horse energy is not about constant motion. It is about knowing when to move, when to pause, and how to stay in relationship with yourself through both.

Closing Perspective

You are allowed to build your year around the body you have. You are allowed to adapt your systems, expectations, and rhythms accordingly. Doing so does not make you less driven, less disciplined, or less capable.

It makes you precise.

And in a Fire Horse year, precision is power.

A Note for the Hard Days

Some days you will not feel reflective, grounded, or particularly interested in growth. You will just feel tired. Irritated. Strained. Or quietly resentful that so much is expected of you. That isn't a moral failure. It's a human one. It's what happens when you are carrying a life.

Hard days do not cancel the work you've done. They affect your mood. They cloud your thinking. They make everything feel heavier than it did yesterday. But they do not erase your capacity. You are allowed to have days when your voice feels faint, when your boundaries soften, when you reach for familiar habits because they cost less energy. That is not regression. That is fatigue.

When you hit those days, lower the expectations, not your standards for how you treat yourself. You do not need a breakthrough. You need something small and honest. A pause before you respond. A decision not to speak to yourself in a way you would never speak to someone you care about. Hard days are not asking you to prove anything. They are asking you not to turn against yourself.

You do not have to rise. You do not have to transcend. You only have to stay with yourself long enough to get through the day without abandoning your own dignity.

And here is the part that matters: the fact that you notice when something feels off is not a setback. It is evidence. Evidence that you are paying attention. Evidence that your internal compass is working. People who are not growing do not feel misalignment. They drift without friction.

So when a hard day arrives, as it will, let it be a day. Not a verdict.

You have lived through seasons that required more than this. You are not beginning from nothing. And this moment does not undo the steadiness you have built.

It means you are alive. You are still aware. You are still in conversation with yourself.

You are not lost in this. You are still here.

Closing Note from Author

We began this almanac talking about circles. Not symbolic ones. Not decorative ones. The real kind. The kind that forms when people decide to stay in relationship with one another, especially when it would be easier not to.

If you've made it here, you already understand that this is not a simple moment to be living through.

There are forces operating right now that are organized, well-funded and explicit about what they want. They are working to narrow rights, restrict autonomy and consolidate power. They are especially focused on women's bodies, labor, safety and futures. Black women. Indigenous women. Women of color, including Latina and Asian women. Disabled women. Queer and trans people. Immigrants. Anyone living at the intersections where power has always been most aggressive.

Naming that isn't pessimism. It's clarity.

This season isn't only about personal growth or learning how to endure. Those matter. But they aren't sufficient on their own. We are living in a time that requires coordination, discernment and relationships that can carry weight without collapsing.

That's where circles matter.

A circle isn't hierarchy. It isn't about performance or looking unified from the outside. It isn't about purity. It's mutual responsibility. It's people adjusting for one another. It's accountability without humiliation. It's care that doesn't disappear when it becomes inconvenient.

That ethic runs underneath this work.

We plan. We build. We stay attentive. We move carefully. We support one another in tangible ways—financially, emotionally, intellectually. We learn when to rest and when to hold a line. We refuse to isolate ourselves just to make survival more manageable.

This isn't about being endlessly strong. It's about being deliberate together.

Hope, here, isn't about positive thinking. It's about practice. It's investing in relationships that last longer than news cycles. It's building trust that doesn't dissolve the first time things get hard. Progress has always depended on people who showed up consistently, even when it was quiet and unglamorous.

If this almanac has offered anything, I hope it has given language to what many of us already feel—the exhaustion, the focus, the refusal to give up on a future that feels more just than the present we inherited. I hope it has made space for uncertainty without asking you to give up your agency.

Whatever this year has been for you, it counts. Not because it was tidy or impressive, but because you stayed in it. Because you paid attention. Because you kept asking yourself what was true.

We are still here. That matters.

You are here. That matters.

And there is still work to do.

What comes next won't require all of us in the same way or at the same time. But it will require relationship. It will require attention. It will require people who are willing to stay present to one another.

Carry that forward. Build carefully. Support generously. Hold each other to standards that make a shared future possible.

I'll be here, too.

— **Tasha**

we are not done yet

Acknowledgments

To the people who steadied me while I pieced myself together—thank you. You may not realize how much of this book you carried with your check-in texts, your dry humor, your "Did you eat?" reminders, or your quiet agreement to sit with me on the days I didn't feel made of much. You showed up in ways that were never performative and always human. That matters more than I can say.

To the ones who remind me I'm not strange for thinking in constellations, outlines, footnotes, metaphors, and color palettes—thank you for letting me be exactly as intense, tender, analytical, political, chaotic, creative, and stubborn as I actually am. You never asked me to shrink. You never asked me to "make it smaller" so you could understand. I notice that. I honor it.

To the women in my life—past, present, chosen, and inherited—you taught me how to hold a line, how to tell the truth without apologizing for it, and how to keep going when the world had other plans. Everything I create has your fingerprints on it.

To the readers who found this book and recognized some part of themselves inside it: thank you. I don't take your attention lightly. I don't take your trust for granted. If anything on these pages helped you feel less alone, less confused, or less convinced that you're "too much," then this book did its job.

To the people who underestimated me—not out of malice, but out of habit—thank you as well. You clarified my direction. You taught me exactly who I write for. (Spoiler: not you.)

And finally, to the version of me who kept writing through chronic illness, grief, exhaustion, economic anxiety, and the constant hum of "Is this worth it?"—I'm glad you never stopped. I'm glad you stayed with the work even when staying felt impossible. I'm glad you believed in a future that didn't exist yet. She made this book possible.

May this work find the people who need it.
May it hold you the way writing it held me.

About the Author

Tasha Monroe is a writer and the creative force behind Simply Edyn & Co., a home for considered living, big ideas and work that tells the truth without theatrics. She writes across poetry, cultural commentary and fiction, following the questions that refuse to be ignored.

Her work explores power, intimacy, womanhood, politics and the practice of staying human in systems that reward performance.

She approaches creativity with discipline and care, building work meant to last rather than work meant to trend.

Tasha believes in discernment over perfection and the quiet strength of a well-placed sentence to move someone forward.

THE CLARITY ALMANAC

www.ingramcontent.com/pod-product-compliance
Lightning Source LLC
LaVergne TN
LVHW090525110826
845146LV00003B/988

* 9 7 9 8 9 9 4 2 6 1 5 0 7 *